New Action Sports

In-Line Skating Basics

by Jeff Savage

CAPSTONE PRESS
MANKATO

C A P S T O N E   P R E S S

818 North Willow Street • Mankato, MN 56001

Printed in the United States of America.

Library of Congress Cataloging-in Publication Data
Savage, Jeff.
    In-line skating basics / by Jeff Savage
    p. cm.
    Includes bibliographical references and index.
    Summary: An introduction to the history, equipment, and techniques of in-line skating.
    ISBN 1-56065-400-7
    1. In-line skating--Juvenile literature. [1. In-line skating.] I. Title.
GV859.73.J39 1996
792.2'1--dc20

                          95-44721
                            CIP
                               AC

Photo credits
Allsport USA: 6, 9, 10, 32, 40
Rollerblade Inc.: 4, 12, 15, 16, 25, 27, 28, 31, 34, 35, 37, 39, 43
F-Stock: 11, 18, 20, 22
Peter Ford: 23

Table of Contents

Chapter 1 Fast-Growing Sport 5

Chapter 2 History 7

Chapter 3 The Skates 13

Chapter 4 How to Skate Safely 21

Chapter 5 Teams and Competitions 33

Glossary 41

To Learn More 44

Useful Addresses 45

Index 47

Words in **boldface** type in the text are defined
in the Glossary in the back of this book.

Chapter 1

Fast-Growing Sport

In-line skating is the fastest growing sport in the world. The popular sport is a cross between ice skating and roller skating.

In 1984, there were only 20,000 in-line skaters in the world. Six years later there were more than 1 million. Today, there are more than 2 million.

In-line skating is also known as blading. Bladers can do many things on their skates. Some of the most popular activities are racing, **cross training**, **extreme skating**, artistic skating, and roller hockey.

In-line skating is the fastest growing sport in the world.

Chapter 2
History

People have tried to skate on wheels for hundreds of years. The first in-line skate was made by a Dutchman in the early 1700s. He nailed wooden spools to blocks of wood and attached them to his shoes.

The skates did not roll well. People had little interest in them.

A Noisy Crash

In 1760, Joseph Merlin, a Belgian musician, tried to impress his friends at a party in

The first in-line skate was made by a Dutchman in the early 1700s.

London, England. Merlin skated into the room on metal-wheeled boots while playing a violin.

He did not know how to steer or stop though. He crashed headfirst into a crystal mirror.

In 1790, a Frenchman named Vanlende invented the ground skate. It had four wheels. The ground skate was used in ballet performances in Europe. It was used at carnivals and other shows, too.

Stopping and steering were difficult. Performers often rolled off the stage into the crowd or into the orchestra pit.

Modern Roller Skating

James Leonard Plimpton is the father of modern roller skating. In 1863, he invented a skate with wooden wheels. He also built the first roller rink in New York City.

By the 1940s, roller skating had become popular. People skated around in a large circle at roller rinks. Other skaters played the smash-up sport of roller derby.

Skates today have urethane or polyurethane wheels.

In-line Skating

In 1980, two brothers in Minneapolis, Minnesota changed skating forever. Scott and Brennan Olson wanted to practice hockey in the summer. They replaced the blades on their hockey skates with wheels made of urethane. Urethane is a hard rubber material. The wheel skates worked.

In-line skaters should always wear knee pads.

Other hockey players soon started using these skates. They were called in-line skates because the wheels were all in a straight line. Before long, there was big demand for them.

The Olson brothers started a company called Rollerblade. People bought the new skates as fast as the Olsons could make them.

Sport Catches On

By 1990, in-line skating had become a popular sport. Rollerblade formed an organization to govern the sport. It is called the International In-line Skating Association (IISA). The group promotes the sport. It sets rules for safety and competition.

Other companies make and sell in-line skates, too. There are newer, faster skates every year.

Skaters swing their arms on an uphill stretch.

Chapter 3
The Skates

The skate has five basic features: a boot, a liner, a frame, wheels, and a brake.

The Boot

Most boots are made of leather, polyurethane, or Kevlar. Some boots are made of all three materials. Boots are also called shells.

There are two separate pieces to each boot. One piece looks like a tennis shoe. It covers the lower part of the foot. The other piece wraps around and supports the ankle.

Standard in-line skates have four wheels.

The liner is the padding inside the boot. It provides comfort and support. It is usually made of foam wrapped with nylon cloth.

More expensive skates use memory foam. Memory foam shapes to your foot as you wear it.

Brake and Frame

The brake is the block sticking out from the heel of one skate. The brake is made of hard rubber or polyurethane. It should never be removed from the skate.

The frame is attached to the bottom of the boot. It holds the wheels in line. It is made of nylon, aluminum, or **titanium**. The frame should be rigid. It should not bend easily.

Wheels

Skates have wheels that are different in number, hardness, and size. More wheels add stability but make it harder to turn. Standard in-line skates have four wheels. Smaller in-line

Advanced skaters prefer harder wheels that spin faster.

skates have three wheels. Racing skates have five wheels.

Wheels are made of polyurethane. Beginners should use softer wheels because they grip the pavement better. Advanced skaters and roller hockey players prefer harder wheels because they spin faster.

Wheel size is measured in millimeters. Beginners should use wheels from 68 millimeters to 72 millimeters in size. Larger wheels, up to 82 millimeters, are faster but less stable.

Types of Skates

Skates are made for different activities. There are recreation skates, racing skates, dance skates, hockey skates, and trick skates.

Racers and advanced skaters use longer skates. Shorter skates are easier to use.

Smart Buying Tips

Buying a pair of in-line skates is not as easy as it sounds. Answer some questions before you buy skates.

Advanced skaters use longer skates.

Have you ever skated before? How much do you weigh? What kind of in-line skating do you plan to do? Are your feet still growing? How often do you plan to skate?

In-line skates are available at most sporting goods stores. Visit a store where someone will spend time with you and answer your questions.

Be sure to buy skates that fit. They should be snug, with solid ankle support. There should be room to wiggle your toes. When trying on the skates, be sure to wear the socks you will wear while skating.

Do not buy cheap or poor quality skates. They do not provide comfort or protection. It is fine to look for bargains, but not at the expense of safety.

Skates should be snug, with solid ankle support.

Chapter 4
How to Skate Safely

In-line skating looks difficult. But it is easy to learn. It just takes some practice. Do not expect to master it in one day.

Beginners can start on grass. Carpeting works almost as well.

To start, put on your skates and walk like a duck with your toes pointed out. Then run. Once you feel comfortable, you are ready for the next step.

Find a smooth, flat area. Pick a place with no rocks, bumps, potholes, or people. Good practice areas are tennis courts and outdoor

In-line skating is easy to learn. It just takes some practice.

basketball courts. Parking lots and schoolyards work well, too.

Posture and Balance

Good **posture** is the key to good skating. Remember the phrase "knees, nose, toes." Your knees, nose, and toes should be in a straight, vertical line when you skate.

Good posture and balance is the key to good skating.

Parking lots and schoolyards are good practice areas.

Try standing with your skates about one foot (30 centimeters) apart. Put one skate ahead of the other. Keep your head up and your eyes on the road. Aim your shoulders and hips straight ahead. Bend your knees. Put your weight on the balls of your feet.

Relax. You are balanced and less likely to fall.

Stroking

Keep your arms in front of you. Gently push off and away from your body with your left foot. Shift your weight to your right foot. Coast on your right foot. As you glide, bring your left foot parallel to and slightly ahead of your right foot.

Now do it the other way. Push off with your right foot. Shift your weight to your left foot. Then bring your right foot parallel to and slightly ahead of your left foot.

Practice these movements over and over again. They are the basic movements of **stroking**.

Stopping

The two basic ways to stop are the **heel stop** and the **T-stop**. The heel stop is the safest way.

The brake on most in-line skates is behind the back wheel of the right skate. To heel stop, extend your right foot forward and lift your

Stroking is a basic movement of in-line skating.

toes up. Your heel will touch the ground. Push down until you come to a stop.

The T-stop is trickier. To do it, keep one foot pointed forward and gently raise the other foot. Place it behind and perpendicular to the forward foot. This forms a T shape. Drag the wheels of the back foot along the pavement until you stop.

Turning

Turning is an important part of skating. There are several ways to turn. The easiest way is to point your skate, lean, and roll in that direction.

The leading skate method is another way to turn. To do it, glide with one skate in front of the other. The front skate will lead you into the turn. If you want to turn left, your left skate should be forward. If you want to turn right, your right skate should point forward. The leading skate method is also called the glide turn.

Never skate without wearing protective gear.

You can also turn by shifting your weight to the edge of the wheels. To turn to the right, place your weight on the inside edge of your left foot. To turn to the left, place your weight on the inside edge of your right foot.

Crossover Turns

Experienced skaters use the crossover turn. They can turn quickly with it. They can also

turn in a fast glide. To do the crossover turn, you balance on one skate while stepping with the other.

To turn right, start into a glide turn. Swing your left foot out, across your right leg. Place your left foot ahead of your right. Then push off with your right foot.

To turn left, start into a glide turn. Swing your right foot out, across your left leg. Place your right foot ahead of your left. Then push off with your left foot.

Skating Backward

Skating backward is challenging and fun. Point your toes inward. Put your weight on the inside edges of your skates. Push outward with both skates. Once you start rolling, bring one foot up next to the other. Repeat again and again. It takes practice.

A wrist guard should have a plastic brace that crosses the palm of the hand.

You must learn to stop while going backward. To do so, use the two-step turn. First, lift your left foot and turn it around. Then place it in line with your right foot, heel to heel. Bring your right leg around to meet up with your left. You then will be headed forward. Stop any way you want.

Safety Equipment

Never skate without wearing protective gear. A full set includes a helmet, wrist guards, knee pads, and elbow pads.

The helmet should be light. It should fit snugly and meet current safety standards.

A wrist guard should have a plastic brace that crosses the palm of the hand. Knee and elbow pads have a hard plastic cup on the outside and a soft cushion on the inside.

All the gear in the world will not protect you if a driver cannot see you at night. Attach reflective tape to your skate boots. It comes in peel-and-stick decals.

Trick skating is called extreme skating.

30

Chapter 5

Teams and Competitions

There are many teams, competitions, and leagues available to in-line skaters. Individual competitions include speed skating, extreme skating, and artistic skating. Cross training and roller hockey are part of team and league competitions.

People at any skill level, from beginner to expert, can participate in leagues and competitions.

There are many competitions available to in-line skaters.

Speed Skating

In-line speed skaters race on an oval track or winding path. The race to the finish line can be a sprint or as long as 100 kilometers (62 miles).

Local and regional competitions are held throughout the United States and Canada. World championships are staged each year in a different country.

Athletes from many sports cross over to in-line skating.

Extreme competition is reserved for advanced skaters.

Extreme Skating

Extreme skating is the display of tricks. It can be practiced on pavement, on steps, and on walls. Sometimes it is performed in contests.

Beginners can practice jumps and spins. But competition is reserved for advanced skaters. The two extreme-skating competitions are streetstyle and **vert** on the **half pipe**.

Streetstyle skaters compete on ramps, pipes, wall rides, and other jumps. Vert skaters do their tricks on a giant half pipe. A half pipe is about 25 feet (eight meters) across and 10 feet (three meters) high on each end. Judges score performances on style, creativity, and difficulty.

Artistic Skating

Artistic skating is like ice skating. Moves are **choreographed**. Some moves are glides, jumps, spins, spirals, and cartwheels. Several moves make up a **routine**.

Individual or team competition is called Hip Hop. Judges score the performances, just like in extreme skating.

Cross Training

Athletes from many sports cross over to in-line skating. They do it to strengthen their muscles and increase their **stamina**.

Surfers, snowboarders, water-skiers, cyclists, divers, and gymnasts train on in-line skates. These athletes form clubs and teams to train together.

In-line skating has something for almost everyone.

Roller Hockey

No other in-line sport has caught on like roller hockey. Leagues are opening up throughout the world. In 1992, roller hockey teams competed for the first time in the Olympics.

Roller hockey is like ice hockey. It is played on a rectangular rink. The weighted puck is plastic. The sticks are wooden. There are five players on each team. Two of them are forwards, two are defenders, and one is a goalkeeper.

Ice hockey must be played on ice. But roller hockey can be played on basketball courts, tennis courts, roller rinks, parking lots, and driveways. It can be played just about anywhere.

Fun for All

In-line skating has something in it for almost everyone. Some people skate for the thrill of acrobatics and the excitement of competition. Others skate simply because they enjoy a fun activity.

If in-line skating sounds right for you, you will be joining millions of people who already enjoy this healthy sport. Just remember to stay alert and skate safely.

Streetstyle skaters compete on ramps, pipes, walls, and other obstacles.

Glossary

choreograph—to design or plan the movements of a dance or other display

cross training—when athletes practice sports other than the one they compete in to improve their performance

extreme skating—display of tricks

half pipe—a concrete structure shaped like half of a pipe on which extreme events take place

heel stop—stopping by dragging the brake on the ground

Millions of people enjoy in-line skating.

posture—the positioning of the body while standing on skates

routine—series of moves

stamina—the strength and energy to remain active and in motion

stroking—pushing off and gliding from skate to skate

titanium—strong, light metal

T-stop—stopping by dragging the wheels of one skate sideways behind the other skate

vert—the extreme competition that takes place on the half pipe

Athletes form clubs and teams to train together.

To Learn More

Brimner, Larry Dane. *Rolling . . . In-Line.* New York: Franklin Watts, 1994.

Feineman, Neil. *Wheel Excitement.* New York: Hearst Books, 1991.

Martin, John. *In-Line Skating.* Minneapolis: Capstone Press, 1994.

Powell, Mark. *In-Line Skating.* Champaign, Ill.: Human Kinetics Publishers, 1993.

Rappelfeld, Joel. *The Complete Blader.* New York: St. Martin's Press, 1992.

You can read articles about in-line skating in *InLine Magazine* and *Speedskating Times*.

Useful Addresses

Amateur Skating Union of the U.S.
1033 Shady Lane
Glen Ellyn, IL 60137

International In-Line Skating Association
Lake Calhoun Executive Center
3033 Excelsior Boulevard
Minneapolis, MN 55416

National In-Line Hockey Association
1221 Brickell Avenue, 9th Floor
Miami, FL 33131

National In-Line Hockey Association Canada
11810 Kingsway
Edmonton, AB T5G 0X5
Canada

Outdoor Marathon Rollerskating Association
P.O. Box 181
Pine Lake, GA 30072

Roll America
240 East 75th Street
New York, NY 10021

United States Amateur Confederation of Roller Skating
P.O. Box 6579
Lincoln, NE 68506

USA Hockey In-line
4965 North 30th Street
Colorado Springs, CO 80919

Index

artistic skating, 5, 33, 36

backwards skating, 29-30
boot, 13-14, 30

cross training, 5, 33, 36

equipment, 19, 30
extreme skating, 5, 33, 35-36

half pipe, 35-36
hockey, 9-10, 17, 37-38

ice skating, 5, 36
International In-line Skating Assocaition, 11

Merlin, Joseph, 7

Olson, Brennan, 9-10
Olson, Scott, 9-10

Plimpton, James Leonard, 8
polyurethane, 13-14, 17

racing, 5, 14, 17
roller hockey, 5, 33, 37-38
roller skating, 5, 8
Rollerblade, 10-11

speed skating, 33-34
stopping, 8, 24, 26
stroking, 24

titanium, 14

turning, 14, 26-27, 29-30

urethane, 9

Vanlende, 8

vert, 35-36

wheels, 7-10, 13-14, 17, 24, 24, 26-27